LADY IN A SUITCASE

Memories Of An Army Wife And Mother

Ilene White

Copyright © 2017 Ilene White

All rights reserved.

ISBN-10: 1976476100

ISBN-13: 978-1976476105

CONTENTS

CONTENTS iii

DEDICATIONS v

THE SUITCASE v

ACKNOWLEDGEMENT v

PREFACE vii

FOREWORD ix

1. EARLY DAYS 1

2. BUILDING A CAREER AND MARRIAGE 5

3. MARRIED LIFE AND THE ARMY 13

4. THE HASH HOUSE HARRIERS 46

5. LIFE AFTER THE ARMY 57

DEDICATIONS

For my husband Johnny, my extended family and friends where ever they are.

THE SUITCASE

The suitcase featured on the cover is Johnny's army suitcase as issued in around 1973 designation CC 8460-99-120-2554

ACKNOWLEDGEMENT

My heartfelt thanks go to Geoff Kirby who has given his help and guidance in compiling and publishing this short book.

DISCLAIMER

Photographs included in this book are believed to be either copyright-free under the Creative Commons Attribution 2.0 Generic licence or permission has been obtained from the owner of the photographs to reproduce them here.

If an image has been used in breach of copyright the author apologizes and will be pleased to acknowledge the copyright holder.

PREFACE

Having recently celebrated her fiftieth wedding anniversary Ilene reminiscences about her childhood and her career in the Women's Royal Army Corps (WRAC). On marrying Johnny in 1964 she embarked on a life offering many adventures mainly based in Germany and the Middle East. In their married life Ilene and Johnny were to live in 16 houses. Despite the travelling and disruption of army life Ilene and Johnny successfully raised two children. Since their retirement they have been enthusiastic Hash House Harriers. Ilene was for several years events coordinator and secretary to the famous Royal Signals White Helmets Army Motorcycle Display Team.

FOREWORD

I joined the Woman's Institute in Weymouth in 2010 over seven years ago, I was a guest of a friend. It was a Fashion Show with strawberries and bubbly.

I thought that sounds like my kind of club. So, speaking to a couple of members of the committee, I was told there was a long waiting list but after chatting said I wouldn't be available for several months in the winter as I usually went to Australia, - so I think I may be the only member who was welcomed immediately – because I couldn't attend regularly.

Two years ago, I was relating a couple of my experiences of life to a friend also from the WI, and she said would I be prepared to do a talk and presentation for them. I thought about it, and said why not? To my surprise it went so well it was suggested I write a book.

So, this is a short story for my family and friends.

1. EARLY DAYS

So, to my story:

Looking back although born in 1943 and we were at war with Germany, I came from a small village called Weeley in Essex quite close to the seaside, (but do not consider myself to be part of the phrase Essex Girl). We were part of East Anglia.

The war didn't appear to touch us very much, but most of our fathers were away fighting, and I didn't see much of mine until I was 7 years old. We didn't appear to go short of anything, we had a large garden all of our vegetables were home grown, we had chickens, a family friend had goats and pigs, so at an early age I grew to love goats cheese.

I am one of 5 girls being the oldest, my father wanted a boy – but after 5 girls my mother said no more! In those days we had a lot of freedom, unlike most children of today.

On summer days, the sun always shined, or so it seemed, we spent most of our time outdoors. My mother prepared a picnic, and friends and I went off on our bicycles or played in the nearby woods in a make-believe world building 'dens' and play acting.

When my father returned from his military service in Palestine, on a warm summers Sunday he would take myself and two sisters (the others weren't born yet) to Walton-on-the-Naze which was only a few miles away.

We went on the train. I remember being at first terrified of the huge steam train as it puffed its way into Weeley station.

We used to find a sheltered spot overlooking the sea, and at lunch time, my father would cut a loaf of bread and we would eat this with fresh salad from our garden and cheese. I was always envious of other people who had the new white sandwich cut loaf but he wouldn't entertain this.

EARLY DAYS

After passing my 'Eleven Plus' examination I won a scholarship and went to a mixed Boarding School in Sonning Common near Reading in the 1950s. The children came from mostly Essex, East Anglia and possibly parts of Hampshire.

We studied hard, but the highlight for me was dance, (Old Time, Ballroom and Latin) which was one of our major subjects. This took place several times a week including two evenings weekdays with just our year group.

Every Saturday night we had a 'Supper Dance' with the whole school, when all the girls dressed up in lovely ballroom gowns and the boys in smart suits.

Later a large proportion of us proudly took our medals, usually Bronze or Silver.

On Friday evenings, it was our Cinema night and the whole school watched a major film in the large Assembly Hall. We had all been to the School Tuck Shop the previous lunch time, so gorged ourselves on sweets and fizzy pop.

All of our parents used to send us two shillings and six pence pocket money per week by Postal Order (equivalent to 12 pence in modern money). This was banked at the School Bank and out of this we had to buy essentials like soap, shampoo and toothpaste, as well as tuck from the shop. Twelve pence does not seem to be very much now, but we could buy a liquorice stick, sherbet dab, and fruit chews, or even fresh fruit for one penny each it did go a long way.

From Monday to Thursday after tea we had an hour of Prep (home work), and then it was on to various activities, two evenings of dance, the other two in the summer mainly outside sports and the winter Guides/Scouts, needlecraft for girls and woodwork for the boys and several other organised activities. Our teachers didn't appear to get much free time.

I enjoyed my school life, I think it had a lot to do with the fact that we were a very small school. There were approximately 30 children (inclusive of the boys) in our year group and each year group, ranging from 1st year to 5th year, from eleven years old to sixteen and we all became close friends; so much so that over the years there have been several reunions and we all remembered each other and had a good time reminiscing.

We had just two classes in the year and I believe not graded, but if

EARLY DAYS

any of us were having difficulty keeping up then those students were taken out of the class to another teacher with no more than six students until they understood the subject, and would then return.

The school dinners for me were very enjoyable, I know some used to complain, but maybe I enjoyed them because my mother was not a good cook (her words).

Twice a term we had what was called 'Visiting Day'. It was usually a Sunday and our parents came to spend the day with us, many travelling long distances. Coaches brought most of them from all over Essex, Suffolk and possibly Hampshire.

We were so excited in the early morning waiting. Some of us used to look out for them at the bottom of the school field and run to meet the coaches as they approached from the main road.

One Visiting Day, my parents were unable to come, so my Uncle came instead. He took me to Lyons Corner House in Reading, where we had high tea. What a treat – to have cream cakes, something we never had at school. I believe there are no longer any of these cafes.

'Rock and Roll' had taken off big time, and all of our school year tried to listen to Radio Luxembourg whenever we could. Bill Haley, Elvis, our own Tommy Steele and my particular favourite Cliff Richard and the Shadows.

Which brings me to an occasion when a few of us got into a corner on the dance floor hoping we wouldn't be seen and tried to do Rock and Roll to a Quick Step tune. Our dancing instructor Mrs Gibbs of course saw us, and said if we wanted to do it then she would teach us properly. It was great fun and we really enjoyed it.

In the school holidays I often went to stay with my best friend from school, Maureen who lived in Ilford.

One evening we went to Ilford Pally. We got up to dance on the crowded floor. We were bemused when we saw the dance floor gradually emptying and there was only us two left. There was a slow handclap, proof that we were doing something wrong. Maureen said

"Don't stop, keep going until the music stops".

We did, feeling very embarrassed. What we discovered was we were doing the ballroom version, which wasn't 'cool'! It didn't take us long whilst watching everyone else to pick up what they were doing.

It taught us not to be so cocky.

We went to the Pally whenever we could in our future school holidays and later. It was a couple of years later that Maureen met on that same dance floor her future husband Ron.

I finished school at 16, thinking I was very grown up, but of course I wasn't.

I went to college in London to do Business Studies & Teacher Training, and two days a week I was loaned to a Company of Patent and Trade Marks Agents in Chancery Lane, this was a small company with only ten of us two of whom were the bosses, the Managing Director only came in occasionally.

As a junior clerk, I learnt so much which helped with my college work. To begin with I travelled to London by train every day. My father used to get me up with a cup of tea in the morning which appeared to be the middle of the night, the train journey was two and a half hours, it wasn't long before I met up with others who were doing a similar thing.

We used to study in the morning and in the evening on our return it was a social time.

After a while the travelling became too much, mainly because trains arrived late in London so I went to live with my Aunty Eileen in Regents Park. It was the time of the early 1960s, Cliff Richard and other bands in 2I's Coffee Bar in Soho, plus other coffee bars with Duke Boxes to dance to, and the local dance Pally's/Clubs (dance halls) the Lyceum Ballroom, also the 100 Club in Oxford Street, and not far from there Ronnie Scott's Jazz Club.

We were what was known as 'the first teenagers' and were having a wonderful time. The music was great, and we followed our favourite singers/bands around - I still do.

After college, I stayed with the Patent Agents, but I wanted to travel. In those days, our parents were happy for us to travel all over The United Kingdom with friends, but going to another country was a different matter. I didn't know about back-packing then and probably wouldn't have been allowed to do it.

2. BUILDING A CAREER AND MARRIAGE

I decided to join the Women's Royal Army Corps (WRAC), as I was told there would be an opportunity to travel.

At the beginning of March 1962, us new recruits all went to Lingfield in Surrey to do a six-week basic training course.

On arrival, we were supplied and fitted with our uniforms and told civilian clothes would not be allowed to be worn until after our training. It meant even when we went out of camp socially we were still in uniform, for me this was very difficult as I loved wearing fashionable clothes.

We learnt how to march (I wasn't very good at this) and we lived in large dormitories. This was very new to most of us, although not so much for me as I lived in one at school.

Some of the girls were very homesick, and wanted to leave. But most of us survived the course, and after we had 'passed out' (graduated) very proudly in front of our families, we were 'soldiers' and then went onto our numerous different trade training, which could have been Drivers, Clerical, Store Women and many more.

This was when we said goodbye to many of our new friends as we went our separate ways, and didn't meet up again.

So, to the travelling which I had so much wanted to do, how lucky I was to go to Germany on my first posting after training. Before this I had to spend three months in Epson, Surrey which was what was called a holding and drafting Unit, (we stayed here before going onto our first Posting abroad. it took that amount of time for me to be what they called 'Positively Vetted', (looking into my background, interviewing my family and friends, and from where I used to work, so I was told) which enabled me to work with Top Secret documents, and in that environment, but I didn't know that at the time.

In that time, most girls waiting to be posted to their first units were employed in various jobs around the camp, I was lucky enough to work in the Telephone Exchange with a retired Colonel, in that time I learnt a lot, and enjoyed it so much I didn't want to leave.

But of course, I couldn't stay.

I travelled to Rheindahlen near Munchen Gladbach, in West Germany, with several other girls which was the Headquarters British Army on the Rhine (BAOR). This was the first time I had been on a plane and travelled abroad, and so was very excited.

I spent two days in transit there and thought that was where I would stay, but that was not to be. Another girl Anne and I had to go in front of the Commanding Officer, and was told we were moving on to a place called Bielefeld, which was Headquarters 1 (British) Corps, and was a top security specialist posting with only 15 female soldiers.

We were given rail tickets and had to travel by train the journey was a few hours, and in that time, we got to know each other, and eventually became very close friends, and are still friends to this day. It was a very new experience for both of us particularly as we didn't speak the language.

When we arrived at the Camp, we were shown to our apartments, which we would be sharing together. We were then told to go to the Cookhouse for dinner, which we did. To our horror when we arrived at the Cookhouse it was just a sea of male soldiers, and most of them stood up and banged their eating utensils on the tables.

We were terrified, left the restaurant without eating and asked to see someone in command. When this was done, we said we wanted to go back to Rheindahlen. It was suggested that we stay for a week and see if we felt differently. We did, and decided we could live with the limitations but we rarely ate in the Cookhouse again when it was full of soldiers.

Fortunately for us our times for finishing work meant we missed the main meal times and the Cooks often did something special for us. Otherwise there was a place just outside the Camp gates called Toc H or the Red Shield (something similar to the Salvation Army), where one could eat and relax where the food was good

BUILDING A CAREER AND MARRIAGE

and not expensive, sometimes because we went so regularly we didn't have to pay, which was just as well, as we were not well paid.

When not working, Anne and I spent our leisure time for the next two years travelling around Europe mainly in a Volkswagen bus. This belonged to an older soldier, we were invited to join him and six other male soldiers of a similar age to ourselves when we were not on duty. So, my ambition to travel was being achieved which was why I joined the WRAC.

It wasn't all fun though. It was the time of what is known as "The Cold War", and my work was heavily involved with this (on the clerical side). The building we worked in was highly secure with armed Guards on each floor. There was serious tension between the West and the Soviet Union (now called Russia).

There was a Code Name 'Exercise Quick Train' where a siren went off and the British military in West Germany had to immediately deploy to their work stations or a designated area, ready to move at very short notice. I remember the siren going off in the middle of the night, this was when the weather was very cold and we had to dress as quickly as possible in our uniform, report to our work stations and wait for the all clear siren. Some of the men in the camp had to be ready to move with their vehicles. Not very pleasant and we were quite scared not knowing what to expect, fortunately it was just an exercise.

We were warned there was always Russian spies of a similar age trying befriend us, and obtain information. We often had instructional films on this subject. This made us very wary when we went out of the Barracks.

One day Anne and I were babysitting for some very close friends. It was very hot and we had the patio doors open. We were talking about our work, when we heard noises outside, and immediately were very frightened because we thought we were being listened to. Of course, we weren't, it was probably just the wind but we never did it again.

Later on, I had to move on from Bielefeld to Sennelager Training Camp about one hours travelling time away. Sennelager was a huge training camp for not only the British but most of Europe. The Unit I was posted to was called 1 War Dog Training Unit, Royal Army Veterinary Corps. It was here I was also put in charge of 12 other girls, in their leisure time and the accommodation we

BUILDING A CAREER AND MARRIAGE

lived in.

I was still on the clerical side; the girls were all Veterinary Staff. They had horses and huge Alsatian dogs to train and look after. I was terrified of the dogs and if any escaped I locked myself in the office. The girls were so brave, as the dogs were very fierce. It was a small unit with only about 30 male soldiers.

The reason why I had the girls under me was the WRAC Sergeant who was also of the same trade as the girls, a Dog Handler, had to unexpectedly move on.

Sennelager had hundreds of male soldiers on the base and also more coming in on a temporary basis, we were the only females, and so were quite vulnerable.

There was one instance where a soldier who probably had too much to drink managed to get into our accommodation one night, he made a quick exit when confronted with all of us girls.

Each night we had a girl on duty and on this occasion, she had forgotten to lock the main door before going to bed. Fortunately for us, the Royal Military Police lived in the next accommodation block, but we found we never needed to call on them, although it was reassuring to know we could.

Before finishing my contract, I met Johnny also in the Army in Germany and he later became my husband.

There was one memorable time – so Johnny says. I didn't drink much alcohol, so when I did it went straight to my head.

We had been to a party and unfortunately I had drunk too much. Johnny had to carry me over the railway lines. I thought he was carrying me over the river - so he says! A German Guard Soldier was looking on in amazement so I'm told.

Fortunately for me none of the girls back in my accommodation saw me, I wasn't setting a very good example. Alcohol, after this, was not for me for a number of years!

Sometime within my service my close friend Maureen (from school days and a civilian) was getting married to Ron.

I returned to England to be her bridesmaid. Johnny (also in England at this time) went to stay with Ron at the apartment Maureen and Ron were going to live in after their marriage.

By this time Johnny had met Maureen's parents, who were my

BUILDING A CAREER AND MARRIAGE

second family since I was eleven years old and treated me as one of their own.

Whilst we were all having dinner a week or so before the wedding Maureen's father asked me what Johnny's name was; up to that time I had always called him "Chalky." He said they wanted to put together the Name Places for the Wedding breakfast.

Sgt. John White (RAOC) in the Trucial Oman Scouts Sharjah 1965-1966

I was puzzled.

"No" he said *"We can't call him Chalky"*.

Johnny then told him his name. I had no idea that Chalky was a nickname for anyone with the surname White, I was so naive in those days. I never called him Chalky again!

In the summer of 1964 we went back to England to get engaged and arranged our wedding date for when I was due to finish my Army career, which would be early 1965, we only signed on for three years in those days.

When we returned to our base in Sennelager Johnny was told he would be posted to The Trucial Oman Scouts in Oman (which is now The United Arab Emirates) for nearly 2 years in January the following year.

I was due to finish in February 1965 and this was when we had planned to get married.

I was also due to go to my close friend Anne's wedding in October (who I served with, she was now back in England having finished her time in the WRAC), but was told I could not take any more leave in England.

I was so upset and disappointed as I was going to be her bridesmaid.

So, we decided to marry in October 1964 the same day as Anne's

BUILDING A CAREER AND MARRIAGE

wedding in Sheffield.

We married in Sennelager, Germany, in a military church on the base, and some of our family and friends from UK were able to join us for the wedding as well as a large number from all over Germany.

Our Wedding Day

We were able to spend a few days after getting married in Amsterdam. On our way we stayed overnight in a hotel on the borders of Germany/Holland. This was the first occasion we had ever slept under a 'Duvet' – it was 'duck down' and so warm and light. This was the first item we brought before returning to England. We went to a hotel which I had stayed in previously on the edge of the Red-Light District, it was used mainly by American Servicemen, mostly on leave after doing a tour of duty in Vietnam.

BUILDING A CAREER AND MARRIAGE

The breakfasts were fantastic – ham, egg and many cheeses, one didn't need anything else to eat until the evening.

When we went back to Amsterdam ten years later, I booked the same hotel. We arrived at night to discover it was now in The Red-Light District and was also a Brothel. I was horrified and refused to sleep on the bed or even clean my teeth, I certainly didn't want breakfast there.

I sat up all night in a chair, because Johnny said it was far too late to attempt to find another hotel. But we did leave as early as possible in the morning!

Our first car which we drove to England and back again when we got engaged was a second hand DKW3/6 (Auto Union) 1958 and now part of the Audi Group. It had many features, a sliding roof, heater which was quite rare in those days, a radio and a three cylinder two stroke engine. A friend said the engine was like a lawn mower.

We loved it.

On my return, to Germany I continued working until just before Christmas. My time had come for me to finish my service. I was offered to extend and take a commission and serve in Aden (the powers that be thought it would be near Johnny who was being posted to Sharjah), I decided that although I had enjoyed my time in uniform, it was now time to move on.

We both returned back to England to spend a month before Johnny left for the Middle East.

We hired a car as we had sold ours in Germany and travelled to Middlesbrough where Johnny's mother and father ran an Off License.

Unfortunately, his mother was very ill and so spent all of the Christmas period in hospital.

Christmas Day, the shop was open for the morning so Johnny and his Dad were working there, I had the task of making the Turkey Dinner and then we would go to the hospital. I could not cook, but had everything prepared and written my timetable out, so was organised, the men closed the shop, came into the kitchen and the food was not even half ready. The clock had stopped! I was so upset I cried.

They were very understanding, and we ended up just having a

BUILDING A CAREER AND MARRIAGE

sandwich. I don't think we told Johnny's mother. When we arrived home late afternoon, we all prepared the dinner to eat in the evening. Not a good start to married life and trying to impress my new father-in-law.

Soon, after Johnny had left the country two of our mutual male soldier friends from Germany were visiting, and rang me up inviting me to go out to dinner in a restaurant. Johnny's father disapproved and didn't think I should go, but with encouragement from his mother I did. I couldn't understand that it wasn't acceptable in his view for a married woman to go out with other men.

I was offered a job in Stockton-on-Tees, but just before taking up the position I was restless and decided that although it was great being with my new family who I loved dearly and particularly my friend and sister-in-law Pat, I wanted to go back to London to my friends. Johnny's Dad was disappointed but his Mum encouraged me saying it was the right decision.

So, it was back to Aunty Eileen's in Regents Park, she spoilt me and I didn't have to do any cooking at all in all my time there. Maybe if I did, it would have prepared me for my life ahead.

3. MARRIED LIFE AND THE ARMY

With gorgeous husband at Mess Dinner in Germany.

MARRIED LIFE AND THE ARMY

Because of my previous service with the WRAC I obtained a position in The Civil Service, Ministry of Defence Department. My work was with The Coldstream Guards in London at Wellington Barracks adjacent to St James Park next to Buckingham Palace. I felt quite at home because although I was now a civilian I was working with the military again, and didn't have to work in the evenings or wear a uniform.

It was a wonderful experience, in my time with them, how exciting to go to events like Trooping the Colour, Buckingham Palace Garden parties and Ladies Day at Ascot. It was a privilege to work in such a wonderful place, and I always got a thrill when I turned up for work, going in the back gate to Wellington Barracks, where the stables were to see the horses being prepared for the parades with the Horse Guards in their splendid uniforms.

The Massed Bands of the Brigade of Guards practicing their wonderful music which later was such a familiar sound but never failed to move me, at the front of the building on the Parade Ground in their red uniforms and big 'Bearskin hats", they looked so handsome.

I used to catch the bus and go down the back roads to my office. When the weather was good in the summer I would walk through St James Park, watching the beautiful pink Pelicans and through to Horse Guards Parade, (where Trooping the Colour takes place each year) then through to St James Palace onto Trafalgar Square and walk to Leicester Square, then would maybe catch a bus or tube to continue on my journey which wasn't far.

How I enjoyed my time working there and was so sorry to leave when Johnny came back and we were posted to the Midlands. In my leisure time, I once again hit the London scene, by going dancing, clubs, theatres, and other city life with friends. I remembered I was married, but of course couldn't stay at home for two years.

It was in the 1960s and the time of the Mini skirt, and London was a very exciting place to be in. I also went back to Germany for a few weeks to help and support my friend with her new baby, her husband was in the military and had to go away.

Of course I did miss Johnny. Phone calls were very rare at that time. We didn't have a phone at Aunty Eileen's and there was the time difference between the countries, so we relied mainly on many letters.

MARRIED LIFE AND THE ARMY

We did manage to spend some time together halfway through his tour, but it wasn't a happy time.

We hired a car and went back up North. His mother was dying of cancer, we were lucky to spend those last few precious hours with her, but she died on our 1st wedding anniversary. Johnny had always been very close to her so was devastated. I felt so sorry that he had to return to his base in the Middle East after his leave and I wasn't there to comfort him.

I did go back up North quite frequently for long weekends or a few days leave. The journey took over 7 hours on the train (now it is only about 3 or 4 from London). I finished work at 5 pm and caught the Pullman Restaurant train, what a luxury to be able to have dinner on board, and to have white tablecloths and be served by waiters. The food was very good too.

I loved the fashions of the day and proudly showed off my mini dresses and trouser suits to my family in the North where that particular fashion hadn't yet arrived. I was stopped by many people wanting to look.

No mobile phones or Wi-Fi so people could see instantly the fashions as now. There was TV but that was still in black and white.

One of my passions were shoes. Because I have such narrow feet it was always difficult for me to get fashionable shoes without paying a lot of money – which I didn't have. I remember a particular favourite was a pair I had made for me, they were in a very pale green, with stiletto high heels and what we called winkle picker toes. To keep the toes in shape and stop them sticking up they were stuffed with cotton wool, not really easy to dance with as they were so long I almost tripped over many times.

Johnny remembers my bright yellow PVC mini raincoat. It always made me smile. I wore it with my long white boots and always felt good, in it, and certainly didn't wait for the rain.

When Johnny had finished his tour of duty, I booked a hotel in St Helier, Jersey for a second honeymoon and long awaited holiday. The hotel we stayed at was quite posh, and dinner was at least 5 courses.

Although very slim I did enjoy my food and the Italian Waiters loved to serve and spoil me, they thought I was too thin. Therefore, they could not understand why after almost a week my appetite

MARRIED LIFE AND THE ARMY

had gone, and I was feeling very unwell most of the time and spent a lot of my time vomiting.

When I spoke to my sister-in-law Pat over the telephone and told her what was happening – she said I was pregnant. How could this be…. Johnny had only been home a couple of weeks. That was how unworldly I was.

Anyway, I was pregnant and was ill for over 5 months. It took me many years before I could look at photos from Jersey, even now if I hear the song 'Yellow Submarine' by the Beatles (who incidentally I love) I begin to feel a little nauseous!

I had a very good friend Susan (who worked in the same department as me) We used to often go to the private grounds in Chelsea to play tennis, and when Johnny was home we often went out as a foursome with John Susan's boyfriend to a restaurant.

When Susan and John got married at the Guards Chapel, a very special place in Wellington Barracks, I went to their wedding, it was quite a grand affair, Susan's father was also Coldstream Guards and he was something to do with the Mountbatten staff, can't remember what but so many people were in full dress uniform.

Our second car was a VW Beetle brought second hand from a friend in Germany. Pauline our daughter didn't sleep very much as a baby at night.

We used to put her in her Carry Cot behind the rear seat of the car and take her for a ride. We wouldn't be allowed to do that now. As soon as we started driving she fell asleep in seconds – but it didn't last, as soon as we put her back in her cot at home she was wide awake again. As a matter of interest as an adult she still doesn't sleep much!

I was what these days is known as a Military Wife. As I said earlier we married in Germany and little did I know then that most of my married life would be spent with a suitcase. Also in the next 30 years or so, I would only spend approximately 5 years in the UK.

Our first posting together was in Chilwell, where we had a Married Quarter but not for long as we brought our first house in Attenborough, Nottingham at a cost of about £3,000 which in those days was an absolute fortune to us, so much so that we dyed sheets to make curtains. I pretended it was cool to make rugs instead of fitted carpets, and had a plastic 3-piece suite, which I

MARRIED LIFE AND THE ARMY

learnt to upholster. We also had a gas refrigerator, the only place they are seen now seems to be in a caravan.

Whilst Johnny was in the Middle East he was earning more money than if he had stayed in UK and this helped enormously with the deposit for our mortgage. The military salary was very small in the 60/70's and to make ends meet several of our men worked at the local Bakery at night.

I worked for a Building Company in Nottingham right up until I was two weeks' overdue from having my baby. My colleagues were very apprehensive because I had become so big, but my only problem was sitting at my desk.

My sister-in-law, Pat came to visit when we were both about 5 months pregnant, and we had eaten between us a large jar of pickled onions. We were so sick, and neither of us were able to look at anything pickled until many years later.

Our beautiful daughter Pauline was born in June 1967 and very soon after the completion on our house was finalised and we were ready to move into our new home in Attenborough just a few miles from Chilwell. Our one luxury which was in the house when we brought it was a telephone, quite unusual at that time, and that was the main reason I went for that particular house, as both our respective families lived so far away.

In our married life, we were to have 16 houses 7 of which were our own.

Two years later Johnny was promoted and again we were on the move this time to Barnard Castle, County Durham in the North of England. We sold our house in the Midlands and brought our second home at great expense or so we thought at that time £4,500. You must realize that our salaries were much less than at today's rate.

It was a brand-new house built for us by Johnny's cousin Eddy who owned a house building company in Marske-by-sea, North Yorkshire, close to all our family.

I lived in it for a short period, but although Johnny was posted to Barnard Castle, he spent a lot of time on exercise in Germany, so it was decided if I wanted to see anything of him I would have to move into Married Quarters in Barnard Castle.

By this time, I was expecting again, and had Jeremy at Catterick

MARRIED LIFE AND THE ARMY

Garrison, North Yorkshire in November 1969.

We put tenants in our house, and, although we had an agent, this did not work

The tenants were not good our rent didn't appear and I had to return to the house in September 1970 when we discovered from our family the tenants were going to do a bunk with all our furniture.

In all the time, they lived in the house, it had never been cleaned, and our neighbour said the tenants came around on their last day to borrow a vacuum cleaner, they had somehow managed to break ours. I arrived at the house in time to stop the furniture van taking our things.

Our first posting abroad was Germany, after being married for six years we decided that we couldn't cope with the hassle of any more tenants and so decided to sell.

So, I moved back and prepared the house ready to sell, we already had a buyer. Johnny by this time had already left for Germany. I was to follow about 6 to 8 weeks later with the 2 children 3 years and 1 year old.

The village we lived in North Yorkshire was not in a military area.

So, one Friday afternoon in thick snow in January I was walking back from the local shops with both children in the pram. I saw an Army Land Rover and somehow knew they were looking for me.

The vehicle was stopped and I was shocked to be handed my Movement Order to fly to Germany on the following Monday from Teesside Airport which was only approximately 30 miles away.

We had no telephone in our house, mobile phones had not been invented and there was a postal strike on. It was the period of unrest within the country with the miners, postal and other workers.

Although we had a buyer for our house, my impending movement to join Johnny so soon was totally unexpected and I could not contact him. My sister-in-law Pat came to the rescue, we contacted the Solicitors who luckily were family friends, and immediately set to work for the Contract to be ready for completion.

To cut a long story short we were ready – house sold. My father-in-law took us to the Airport his last words were

MARRIED LIFE AND THE ARMY

"Don't worry you are now in the Army's hands, they will look after you."

He was ex-RAF so he knew these things!

Famous last words...

We arrived at RAF Gutersloh, West Germany to find nobody waiting to pick me up, or even expecting us. It was then I realized Johnny did not know I was coming. A message was to be left for him at his Unit, which fortunately I did know.

I had no address to go to apart from his Unit which was 26 Engineer Regiment in Hemer, Near Iserlohn. We were then put in an Army coach by ourselves with luggage and a German driver who did not speak English, and travelled the long journey, fortunately I did speak enough German to get by.

We had been going some distance in thick snow when we came to an area with houses – and somehow I knew I had almost reached our destination.

I told the driver to stop – and who should be coming out of a house was Johnny – a few more minutes and I would have missed him. He had only just discovered a few hours earlier because of my phone call that I had arrived and was on my way because of the phone call.

He managed to borrow food, blankets etc to welcome us to an empty apartment. Jeremy slept on two arm chairs put together that first night.

We spent the next three happy quite uneventful years in that location, I was able to get employment within the military barracks and teaching commercial subjects. Once again we had a good social life. After our first year 1972 we decided we needed to buy another house in the UK. House prices were rapidly rising and we knew if we didn't get back on the house ladder now we would not be able to later.

Johnny sent me home with Pauline to house hunt, and he took leave and looked after our son.

We decided to go back to the same village in the North East because that's where Johnny's family were. As it was we could not afford to buy a house in the same estate as our previous one, and so had to look elsewhere.

Again, we put tenants in, and hoped we would not have too many problems with them. Although we once again had an agent, we had made friends with our neighbours who said they would keep an eye on the house for us. Incidentally, every house we brought was by me Johnny was always abroad at the time.

Our next posting was Iran, what an amazing place, we moved there in 1974, it was the time of the Shah before he was over thrown in 1979.

My journey was on a BAOC (now British Airways) VC10 aircraft which wasn't without incident, it should have been a seven hours' journey but in fact was more like fourteen.

What nobody knew at the time was War had just broken out in Cyprus the Turks had invaded, Airspace was closed so the journey was diverted several times. One at Damascus where several armed police boarded the aircraft which was quite frightening.

We eventually landed in Tehran in the middle of the night and I remember getting out of the plane thinking I was walking into a hot oven. We were met by a very anxious husband who up to that time had no idea what had happened to us.

Our swimming pool in Iran

MARRIED LIFE AND THE ARMY

We lived in a very large apartment on the edge of a mountain with a garden and a large swimming pool. The swimming pool was 6 ft deep, so we thought it better to fill it immediately and teach the children to swim, rather than fall into an empty pool.

The Iranian government had brought British Tanks and Johnny was part of a military team of 15 commissioning and advising on their arrival, etc. The military team was called Commissioning and Advisory Team (CAAT) Iran included was the Military Attaché, I worked for the British Embassy, which we were all part of.

We brought our food mainly from the local community, the Bazaars etc, we did also buy from the Supermarkets but this was very expensive. My memories are of buying chickens in the bazaars which I had to cut off the heads and take the insides out.

Yuck...

Soon after my arrival we were invited to our Landlord and lady for tea. Tea is very popular in Iran, and consisted of cucumber, dates and nuts and tea. They had a grown-up daughter and son Johnny had never seen the daughter until that day, as he was a single man at the time daughters were not seen outside their immediate family.

She was very beautiful. So was the son, although he had a lot of facial hair. The wife was showing us family photos and there was one of Homi the son, who was clean shaven, I outspokenly said I preferred him clean shaven. The following day he met up with me with a big smile without his beard and moustache, and in my opinion looked very handsome.

The wife at tea had a beautiful pair of Iranian embroidered slippers on. I admired them and immediately she took them off and gave them to me. Johnny said I should have admired the carpet.

We had quite a long driveway from our house to the road and each morning I walked with our children Pauline and Jeremy, for them to catch their private bus to Rustan Abadian an English teaching school. Several of the extended Royal family children also went to the school, so ours were lucky enough to occasionally go to parties at the palaces, and as parents we were invited also.

For some time, we were aware that a large dog was following us each morning.

MARRIED LIFE AND THE ARMY

It gradually came closer as time went on, so we started feeding it, realizing it was a stray and was hungry. The dog has such long hair, the only way we knew where his face was, was when he was eating.

Our acquired dog 'Scruff'

So, we called him 'Scruff', eventually he started to follow the children to the house, so it was decided that if he was going to adopt us then he should have a bath (he was filthy and very matted).

We tried but were unsuccessful, so took him to one of the few dog parlours in Tehran. We took him very early in the morning, and was getting quite concerned when most of the day had gone with no phone call to say he was ready for collection. When we did get the call, we were told we would have a surprise.

Yes, we did as they had shaved him completely, and we had in front of us a beautiful black full sized Poodle, his coat was like velvet. He still had a long tail and a white bib, and we still called him 'Scruff' and he became a very good house dog. He adored the

MARRIED LIFE AND THE ARMY

children and us all.

One day I decided to take the children for a walk up the mountain, we came to a village, and unfortunately we were foreign and so were not welcome, and as we approached the centre we were 'stoned' a young Iranian came to our rescue and escorted us back down the mountain.

I had to tell Johnny and he was not happy that I had risked myself and the children's life and of course mainly because I had not told anyone where we were going!

The Gruesome Festival of Ashura

In October, there was a big Islamic festival that happened every year. It's called 'Festival of Ashura' which left a huge impression on me.

It is where Shiite Muslims gather to commemorate the death of Prophet Muhammad's grandson.

They beat themselves with knives, chains and swords until they draw blood. I know it goes on in other parts of the world but I was unaware of it, and haven't seen it since.

Recently an Iranian friend told me that the practise has now publicly been banned in Iran.

MARRIED LIFE AND THE ARMY

Our overland trip in Iran

These places I am going to talk about may not be in the correct order, as it was so long ago I cannot remember.

We did a journey with the children leaving Tehran (where we lived) in our car, which Johnny drove out from UK to Iran. But that's another story.

We drove to Hamidam where among other things they made beautiful glassware and turquoise jewellery, miniature painting done in watercolours on camel bone.

After Hamidam we stayed overnight in a Caravansary in very basic hotel and eating the local food with our fingers no knives or forks, but you could almost imagine the camel trains with the Nomads coming through. Which I believe they still did on their way to other trading ports

We later went through a very steep mountain pass, where the car at some points was almost on the edge of the narrow and dangerous mountain road the drops each side were terrifying.

We had been driving for about 2 ½ hrs in searing heat (no air conditioning in cars in those days) when I asked Johnny how far we had travelled – he said 15 miles – I didn't ask again!

The steep mountain pass

It was worth the experience for at the bottom of the terrain we came across a village of Nomads.

Their homes were black skin tents.

Black skinned Nomad tents

MARRIED LIFE AND THE ARMY

Nomadic mother and child

It was as if we were going back over 2,000 years in Biblical times. There were sheep around peoples' necks, their clothes were very basic and chickens all over the place. I was concerned because I had never seen people like this before, and they were fascinated by our children., and kept wanting to touch Jeremy who at the time had blonde hair.

Next we came to a plateau of people and caves where their homes were in Caves and the people dressed in beautiful coloured clothes men and women. We stopped to eat, the local food and our children were welcomed and made pottery.

Cave houses in Iran

MARRIED LIFE AND THE ARMY

Colourfully dressed nomadic women

Later we went to a very religious place called Qom where the Mosques were in Gold.

MARRIED LIFE AND THE ARMY

Qom's main mosque

We came across a funeral of a young boy, where men and boys only were marching in columns, there was a big poster of the boy there was no sign of any women.

We weren't welcome so did not linger.

I have been told by an Iranian friend that Qom is the equivalent to our city of Canterbury and is very famous for its religious festivals.

MARRIED LIFE AND THE ARMY

Persepolis

Then on to Persepolis built by Darius The Great it was the capital but then destroyed by Alexander the Great in 323 BC.

Persepolis

We spent an evening there and watched a 'Sound & Light' performance which in-acted the battle between Darius and Alexander. It was so realistic the children were terrified and hid under the seats. We had to take them back the following day to show it really was just a historic ruins site, and we had been watching a show. How amazing it was!

We then went onto Shiraz which I believe may have been the capital in 16th/17th century. It was a beautiful Garden City with bright flowers everywhere.

Gardens in Shiraz, Iran

The Central Mosque in Shiraz, Iran

MARRIED LIFE AND THE ARMY

The Vakil Bath in Shiraz, Iran

Then onto Esfahan which I believe was the most beautiful city in Iran. The Mosques were mainly in a beautiful shade of turquoise as they were in Shiraz and many other cities in Iran.

The Mosque at Esfahan

We watched while exquisite carpets and metal plates were beaten by hand into patterns and shapes and were being made by hand in the Bazaars. I don't know why we never brought a carpet while we were there maybe because they wouldn't fit in our English homes (and maybe we couldn't afford them either).

MARRIED LIFE AND THE ARMY

Also, there was the most amazing passages inside the Bazaar, filled with shops of Gold, jewellery being made and sold, the smell of many spices, and incense.

A typical handicraft shop in a Bazaar

MARRIED LIFE AND THE ARMY

Enough of this journey which lasted just over a week.

There was a memorable time when the team had gone to the Airport to pick up our food supplies which came from the British base in Cyprus. It was probably January a period of deep snow.

Possibly the only time I can say a glass of beer possibly saved their lives.

The RAF flight had been delayed because of the bad weather, so the team (15) were in the bar upstairs. They heard a terrible crash, and through a side door saw the roof go down past them into the Arrival Lounge.

There was a terrible silence, snow coming in, a guard trapped in the door jam.

The devastating airport roof collapse. Johnny's location circled.

Our team were able to rescue him. I believe there were many casualties.

Our team were in uniform, but no one was hurt they were safe, but somewhat shaken.

MARRIED LIFE AND THE ARMY

The devastating airport roof collapse. Johnny's location circled.

They were told to leave immediately by the RAF Liaison Officer to go home there was nothing they could do. One of them managed to get to a telephone to forewarn us wives on what had happened to expect them back in some state of shock.

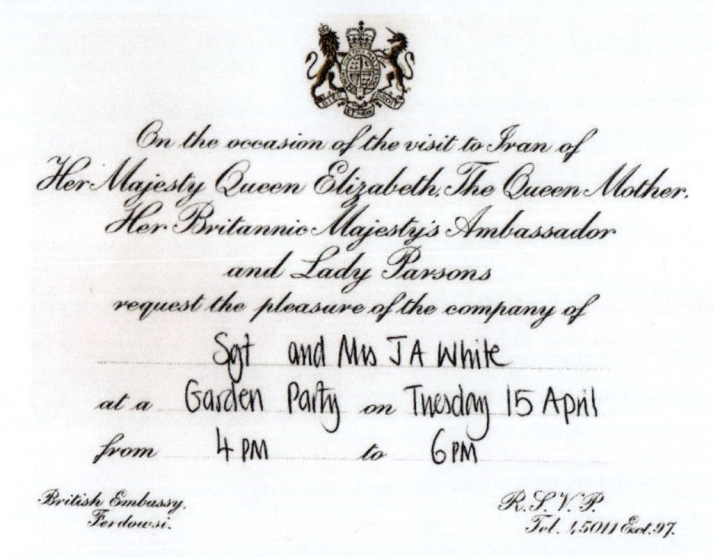

On the occasion of the visit to Iran of Her Majesty Queen Elizabeth, The Queen Mother. Her Britannic Majesty's Ambassador and Lady Parsons request the pleasure of the company of Sgt and Mrs J A White at a Garden Party on Tuesday 15 April from 4 PM to 6 PM

British Embassy. Ferdowsi.

R.S.V.P. Tel. 45011 Ext. 97.

Our invitation to meet Elizabeth the Queen Mother

We frequently went to receptions and cocktail parties at the British Embassy, which we were part of. There was a particular reception when we were each introduced to The Queen Mother when she visited. It was such an honour when she spoke to each one of us.

The Shah and family

The Shah fled in 1979 a of couple of years after we left, fortunately or we could have been one of the people who were in the American Embassy when it was stormed. The military team that took over after us were there.

Back to Germany again for another 3 years but this time a different location in a place called Osnabruck.

We had only been there seven months when Johnny got promoted and it was time to move on again, still in Germany, but many miles from Osnabruck in Viersen on the German/Dutch border.

Now we had to make a huge decision concerning the children's education.

Pauline by this time had already attended seven schools, and Jeremy five and it was affecting their education.

MARRIED LIFE AND THE ARMY

The Army school that Pauline was attending believed in progressive education at that time, a huge classroom, where they could learn if they wanted to.

A friend who was also a teacher said he believed Pauline should attend a Boarding School, such a hard decision, but we decided if one went they would both have to go.

How we hated that decision, as much as our son Jeremy did, and he never really enjoyed that period of his schooling. But he did give us some stories to dine out on.

We were taking the children to a small airport in Germany to attend school in England, when the children had left us and we were watching through the glass windows.

They were ready to take their luggage into the chute, when Jeremy dropped his passport down the chute, so promptly went down after it!

We did see him climb back up with his passport intact.

The next I will relate later...

Our next posting, we went to Kuwait, joining a British military team called The Kuwait Liaison Team, because we were supplying the Kuwaitis Government with British Army equipment mainly tanks, we were there at the time when Iraq invaded Iran.

We stayed in Kuwait for approximately 3 ½ years. There were a few problems in Kuwait at that time but we really weren't too involved.

We lived in a very large apartment in the town of Salmiya just a block from the sea and a few kilometres from Kuwait City. The bulk of our military team and wives and young children lived in a complex called IBI in Fahaheel, this was also our recreation area with a swimming pool and clubhouse.

As there were so few of the military personnel particularly those living in town, most of our friends were from the civilian expat community. Particular friends of ours were Jenny, Roy and their two very young daughters. We spent a lot of time with them, and when I was working Johnny helped Jenny with the children and take them to the beach most days, they were joined by our Pauline and Jeremy when they were home in the holidays from boarding school.

Jenny was not a good cook (her own admission) and I often used to go to their home to rescue the food. We are still friends and this summer we spent a few days with all the family, the girls now grown up with their husbands and young children. We didn't eat at Jenny's so I don't know if she can cook now!

A favourite pastime was going down to the local beach in Salmiya and watching the boatmen launching their boats from the slipway with a car. More than once the handbrake would be left off and the car would follow the boat into the water.

The Kuwait Towers

I worked in Kuwait two jobs really. A friend asked me if I would take on the secretarial appointment of his company, a major Town Planning project overseen by the Kuwait Government. I worked from 7 am to 2 pm, quite normal hours because the afternoon heat was so intense, although most places had air conditioning but outside in the summer the temperature could reach 50 degrees.

The Company were designing a new town and road system for the district of Hawali.

The characters who worked there, architects, and designers were very colourful and came from different countries and cultures. They could on occasions be very temperamental.

Going to work was quite hazardous. I always booked the same taxi driver, it was too dangerous driving in the rush hours the traffic was mad and so much of it. Being a single female I had to sit in the back and the driver insisted on having a conversation with me which was good, but he always turned around to look at me and not the road. How I survived those journeys I don't know!

My second job: I had been to a reception at the British Embassy, and was approached by someone who had been told I was also a Commercial teacher and she wanted to learn to type.

I eventually reluctantly agreed if she could find at least five others who wanted to learn but to supply their own typewriters... So, that is how my own school of Typing and English Grammar was started for expats two afternoons a week on our huge dining room table.

It became very popular with many more students, and I ended up having to travel to another venue, buying more typewriters to meet the need and made many friends. Johnny had to transport everything our car, fortunately we did have a large car.

The Royal Yacht Britannia

MARRIED LIFE AND THE ARMY

We were honoured to be introduced to Her Majesty the Queen and entertain the Royal Yacht Britannia crew when the Queen visited the Amir on an official visit to Kuwait, she quite often used the Royal Yacht as her official residence as she did on this occasion.

Our team had the job of feeding some of the crew at our own homes, and were later entertained on board the Royal Yacht, which was a huge honour.

Ready to meet The Queen!

Every year Rothmans (the cigarette company) did their Motor Rally through the desert. We were designated as Marshalls. On our first year, on convoy we were following the guide through the deserted desert, where at each check point one car was dropped off and then we continued on until it was our turn. We were left in the middle of nowhere, and then had to set up check points and camp.

Marshalling for the Rothman's Rally

Marshalling for the Rothman's Rally

We were going to be staying overnight, and only had the car no tent. It was very windy and the wooden stakes had to be dug into the ground. Johnny left me holding one while he went to another area to insert another one. When he looked around I had vanished. The wind had taken the stake and I had to go running after it as we hadn't anymore!

Night time in the desert gets very cold. We had some wood to keep the fire going, but ran out, so Johnny collected camel dung, which gave us a lovely fire.

The next evening after the Rally was over we were all invited to a ball. Quickly showered and changed, and couldn't understand why no one wanted to be near us....... The camel dung had impregnated itself into our skin, and we smelt terrible!

Our children were well used to Boarding School by this time, although Jeremy was still unsettled, and it was always a problem when it was time to return to school after the holidays, which were always spent with us, they were much longer than state schools.

Two things stick in my mind.

The day before he was due to return to school was always a little tense and on this occasion, he had gone to bed but on his door was a large notice to say

Johnny, Jeremy and Pauline.

"I'm not going to school tomorrow"

He had gone to bed quietly so we thought he had got it out of his system. But no, the following morning he came into our bed as he always did. Johnny went to get his school uniform which had been prepared the day before, and couldn't find it. Eventually it was found, Jeremy had hidden the uniform at the bottom of the laundry basket which was full of other clothes.

MARRIED LIFE AND THE ARMY

One memorable journey was at a Christmas time. Johnny went to collect Jeremy from the Airport, while I took Pauline who had arrived a few days earlier to a party which was about one hour's drive from our house. He would meet me at the party with Jeremy or if not there I would drive home. Which I did. On arrival, there was Johnny but no Jeremy.

"Where is he?" I asked.

"I don't know!" he said.

There were no telephones so we couldn't ring anyone. I spent the worst night of my life. Johnny went to the Airport very early next morning, in uniform and Jeremy was there.

Apparently, the weather had been so bad in Yorkshire that the teachers decided to put him on board a flight to Kuwait from their local airport which was Leeds/via Paris and then on to Kuwait. But they hadn't informed Heathrow, so no one knew where he was.

He spent 8 hours in Paris, where he was taken around by we believe a member of the crew and shown the sights, thoroughly enjoyed himself, and then put on the plane to Kuwait. After that I insisted we have a telephone installed. Another occasion I had a call from him. He was possibly 12 years old. I asked if he was back at school.

"No" he said, *"I am at a hotel in London, because the plane was late the teachers hadn't waited"*.

I asked if he was going straight to bed.

"No", he said *"I am going to watch the films all night."*

When he was 16 he told me that on that occasion he travelled across London by himself and caught the train to York again by himself and got a taxi to school. Fortunately, he always had money with him.

For me having the children in Boarding school was the most difficult part of our Service life, but if I had returned to England by myself to live, Johnny only had leave to UK once a year so the children would see so little of him, but this way the children spent so much time with both of us, I returned to England by myself never with Johnny so that we could spend even more time with them. Their half-terms were spent with Johnny's family who acted as surrogate parents for us.

MARRIED LIFE AND THE ARMY

A Typical Dust Storm about to envelope an army camp.

Dust storms were frequent in the summer months in Kuwait. These are like a very thick fog and you can't see more than a few metres ahead of you. Also, the sand gets everywhere in your eyes and throat. We once got lost on the way home from an evening event at an area we knew well – but we lost all sense of direction.

You can't believe how cold it gets, the temperature can drop from 100 degrees to 70. On our first winter, we saw other expats wearing winter clothes and couldn't believe it.

"You wait until next winter" they said.

Yes, we were wearing winter clothes the following year, and I was in tights! We needed fires in our houses to keep warm, as our soldiers found out when the Gulf war was on.

After Kuwait we returned to England. Our first time living in the country for many years. It was good to catch up with friends we had almost lost touch with. Johnny was posted to Donnington, near Telford in Shropshire. I stayed in our house in Marske-by-sea which was quite novel for me.

We had become very close friends with Johnny's boss from previous days in Vierson, West Germany Captain McClosky and his wife Dot. When Captain McClosky finished his Army career he gained a position at Windsor Castle as a Superintendent Clerk. This meant he and his wife lived in an apartment at Henry 111's

MARRIED LIFE AND THE ARMY

Tower. Johnny and myself were invited to stay on several occasions. How exciting! We used to stand on the balcony to listen to the Guards Bands down below us. We were told not to wave at people in case they thought we were Royalty. We were permitted to walk in the Queen's private gardens and I remember we opened the gate with a very large key.

Many of my friends and family know I am claustrophobic, I usually manage this well, and the condition has never stopped me doing anything. If a hotel we are booked in has more than 6 floors I request in advance a lower floor, as I am unable to go in a lift or a confined space. Sometimes this is an issue particularly if abroad in a foreign country, because the stair case in the main hotel area does not always go above the 3rd floor. My request isn't always taken on, I then have to be escorted through a back fire escape with a bell boy or someone similar. I have happily walked up 15 flights of stairs. My claustrophobia I believe was started after I became trapped in a lift in Nottingham when I was expecting Pauline our first child more than 50 years ago.

There was one memorable time. Our first grandson James had been born in Australia. Jeremy rang me and said he had booked me on a flight to Sydney. Belinda and himself wanted me to meet James whilst he was only just over a week old.

I said: 'What by myself'

'Yes', he said.

Anyway the following day he rang again and said he had managed to get a flight for his Dad also – but we would be on different aircrafts – but on the same day.

Pauline and Richard took us to Heathrow, we were going to be in different terminals. I later found out they deposited Johnny first so they could stay with me, and make sure I couldn't change my mind about going. I hate flying!

I was flying Singapore Airlines and have an issue with toilets on board, if the door closed whilst I was inside then I would panic. We have always got around this because Johnny would put his fingers inside the door so it wouldn't close.

The lovely stewardess came over to me and quietly said:

'When you want to use the toilet, please let me know'. This worked very well for me.

MARRIED LIFE AND THE ARMY

When we were due to leave Singapore on the second leg of our journey we had a crew who were all male.

A steward came over to me and said in a **very loud voice:**

'When you want to use the toilet Mrs White, please let me know' – of course all the people around me knew also.

4. THE HASH HOUSE HARRIERS

Hashing - No Tunnel Left Unexplored!

This is where I will come to Hashing. I am a Hash House Harrier and have been for almost 40 years. So many people ask me what this means. So, I thought I would tell you a little of who and what we are. Not only do we run, we cycle, walk long distances, we are very socially motivated, like to party, and need to be a little eccentric to participate.

We are part of an international group of non-competitive Cross Country Runners. I am not going to go into the history, it would take too long, but just to say it was started in 1930s by some Expats who wanted to get fit. They started at a "Hash House Restaurant so called because the food was not good, in Kuala Lumper Malaysia, and of course Harriers is self-explanatory. It is based on paper chasing 'Hare and Hounds'.

THE HASH HOUSE HARRIERS

Hashing stopped during the Japanese occupation World War Two, and was resurrected again in the 1960s in Singapore, and quickly spread throughout the World with like-minded people.

I currently belong to the Weymouth Group which is Hardy Hash House Harriers, there are about 40 registered members but usually on our Sunday turnout (which is every Sunday incidentally), we get about 20 sometimes more, particularly if it is broadcast there will be a party later in some one's house, we are all very supportive of each other, and like one big family.

Before I joined in Weymouth, I started abroad, when Johnny was in Oman with the Sultan's Forces, it was a good way to have a social scene and of course keep fit. Many a time I have turned up at an airport on a birthday or special occasion to be met by Johnny with my hashing kit and trainers, and told right we are running up that mountain or terrain – and thinking what am I doing here – but then the parties are worth it.

A Hashing Party in the 1990s!

Because - yes - we are party animals, and need to be a little crazy to join this group. We have run in so many countries all over the world approximately 12, included in those are several cities within those countries, including of course all over the UK, and the Channel Islands.

We all have nick names, (mine is 'Clipboard', so called because I was always organising something). We sometimes never discover the original names of our fellow Hashers, we can be from all walks of life from someone who sweeps the road to top business people and politicians. Again we don't always know, nor do we care.

Sometimes it does get a bit risqué, but if one doesn't like it we just walk away. Hashing caters for all levels of fitness. But I must say we all start off as runners.

We are non-competitive, and follow a trail (you may have seen it) usually of flour or sawdust, in hot countries usually paper. In fact, talking of paper that it what it is based on. The old-fashioned Paper Chase. Usually, we run about 6 to 7 miles but could be more if the front runners take a false trial and have to come back, but that gives the slower runners time to catch up.

We have re-groups once again to allow the slower ones to catch up. Normally it is cross country running which could end up going across rivers, or thick mud, some like it the dirtier the better, hence some children love it. Ours did, and so does our granddaughter.

An International Hashing Event in Brussels

THE HASH HOUSE HARRIERS

Over 5,500 Hashers from around the world did a charity 'Red Dress Run' around Cardiff in 2004.

We don't tend to advertise, Hashing is spread by word of mouth, but is also big on the various websites.

In England, we became part of the Wessex Hash House Harriers and were lucky to have known some of their members abroad, so we already had friends. Later we moved on, to Weymouth.

We don't often do Charity events, except each time we have an International Hash, Euro (European) or every second year somewhere in UK which is called our Nash (National) Hash. The charity event is called a Red Dress Run, men and women all get dressed in Red dresses, and run through the designated city running the Hash.

We all pay extra to go on this event, and it is always on a day or so prior to the main events. You may have seen this happen in Weymouth because in 2013 the Hardy Hash hosted and organised the Nash Hash, where we had 500 Hashers (they don't like to be called runners).

The Red Dress Runt is an amazing sight to see. The money collected, which is quite considerable goes to a local charity of the organizers choice.

Dressed as Oompa Loompas in Brussels for a Hashing event

Any opportunity a Hasher has to put on Fancy Dress then they are in their element.

One occasion, we were on an excursion for the day to a Cider Festival in Bath, there were 30 of us. We caught an early morning train, on a Valentine's Day, so we were dressed in red and hearts etc.

We had the first carriage.

We played pass the parcel – we suspect the organiser of the game had previously chosen his victims for the forfeits with care.

A young lady was given the task – when the train stopped at the next station, she was to get off, give the first man a hug and say:

'I Love You'

then get back on the train. Well she did – if you could have seen the look of bewilderment on the young man's face, then a huge grin it was hilarious. Whether he did get on the train we don't know.

In 1986 Johnny had returned to UK after completing his first tour of Oman and went to work at what he knew best the British Army in Bovington Army Camp. In 1989 an American Muscat Hasher John Dorr had finished his contract in Oman and was returning back to his home in America via UK. He got in touch with twelve of us and we met up in a hotel in Diss, Norfolk. We had such a good time so we did it again the following year but this time in the Midlands and without John. We did do a run, so I am reminded by Rick but only around the hotel grounds.

On that weekend it was decided that we would form a reunion – so it was how the Muscat UK Hash House Harriers {HHH} Reunion was formed. I was voted in as Hon Sec and my first task was contacting others who had returned from Oman or were due to return.

Hotels were expensive so a decision was made to camp and hold a communal Bar-be-que at a different location every year as we did in our parent hash. After five years Tony Fellows joined us and became our first Grand Master.

I continued as Hon Sec for approximately 20 years until work commitments and travelling made it too difficult (Johnny by this time had gone back to Oman on a second contract to work again with the military, but mainly Americans, in a place called Thumrait).

We recently celebrated our 30th year of the reunion and had seventy-three members attend in the New Forest. Some of these from all over the world and four still serving in Oman joined us. I remember we started off with the tents, now there are quite a number with caravans or motor homes. I wonder how much longer we will manage to go on!

Every two years there is an International Hash which many of us from the Hardy Hash go on, Johnny and I try to go as often as we can, where we eventually meet up with sometimes 5000 to 6000 people from all over the world, many friends who we only meet up with on these occasions.

Of course, there isn't just one trail to follow on these occasions but we are usually bussed out to several venues to choose from about an hour's plus journey, which means we see more of the country we are visiting.

If we travel abroad on holiday we normally take our hashing gear, and join a local Hash whether it is Australia, New Zealand or the Middle East. We are always welcome wherever it is.

With Hashing friends in Chiang Mai

Participating in a charity 'Red Dress Run'

THE HASH HOUSE HARRIERS

If I can tell you about one of my favourites it was the 2006 Interhash in Chiang Mia (Thailand) where we would all eventually meet up.

But because the main Hash only lasts usually 3 days most of us would not travel long distances to just go on that – so they have what is called a pre-hash and a post-hash.

This particular one (and they usually follow a similar pattern) started in Singapore, where the local Hash set the trial, through forests etc, where we encountered monkeys in the trees.

I had an exhausting run, and then party through the night. A very early start where about 400 of us caught the 'Hash Train' at Singapore station, we were met by Chinese Dragons to wish us luck.

We were greeted by a Chinese Dragon at Singapore Station

We would then travel for almost a week, through different parts of the Malaysian Peninsular, stopping at Kuala Lumper overnight. Next day onward to George Town for an overnight stay to Hash in Penang.

THE HASH HOUSE HARRIERS

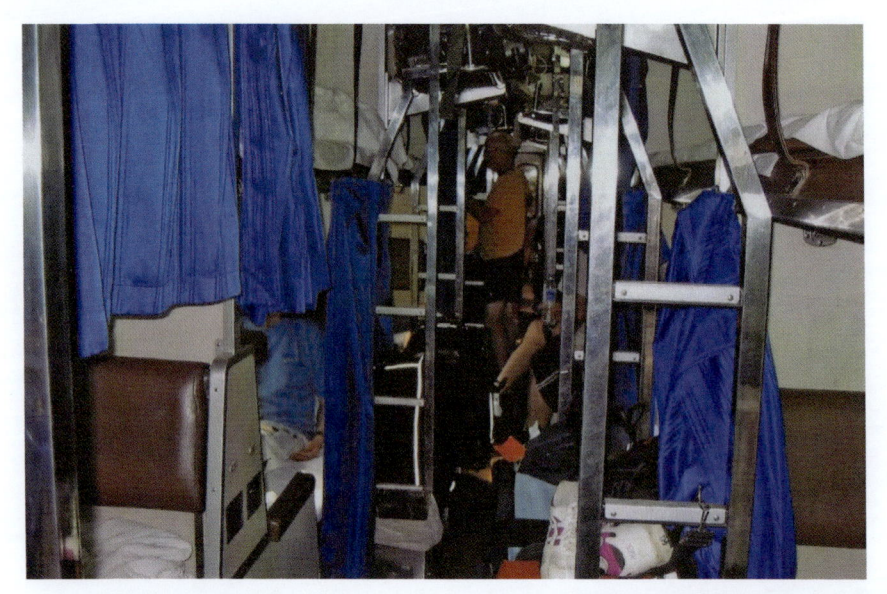

The crowded sleeping compartment on the 'Hash Train'.

The following day we went on to Northern Malaya then into Thailand, including Bangkok, the 'Red Light' district, getting off the train, running again through set trails such as paddy fields, and other places tourists rarely get to see, partying (maybe), then getting back on the train to sleep, after going to the venues by coach, or staying overnight in a hotel.

A typical street scene in Chiang Mai

THE HASH HOUSE HARRIERS

We did a Hash through the Red Light district of Bangkok, a friend and I were persuaded by one of the local Thai girls in a club to do a Pole dance, we did but stopped when we realized a man was trying to put money in our shorts. This was on our wedding anniversary, needless to say `Johnny was somewhere else in the district at that time...

Each time we were welcomed by local people and children with garlands, sweetmeats, and music. Why? Because we brought trade into their areas.

After Chiang Mia where there were 6000 of us from all over the world, 400 of us then went onto Vietnam, where we did the same again, Hanoi, South to Da Nang, then south to Ho Chi Min City, (old Saigon), and three other venues by air. On one of these trips we had a banquet on a steam boat. Not many of the locals joined us and we were told later they didn't trust the boats as they quite often sank. We weren't aware of this so had a good time anyway.

Then it was the end of our trip, back to Bangkok, for most of us, and onward to UK, for our UK Hashers to rest, but not yet for us, after spending more time in Bangkok this time to relax and see the sights with a couple of friends, The River Flower Gardens, Bridge over the River Quoi, and the famous night markets. Whilst in Bangkok Isabel and I went to the Night Market and came back on a Tuk Tuk.

With a friend riding a Tuk Tuk in Bangkok

A friend had warned Isabel not to go without a male, because of

THE HASH HOUSE HARRIERS

possible kidnaps. The traffic in Bangkok is crazy and our driver had no respect for it and crossed on the main highway in front of traffic in both directions barely missing them. He then took us down very dark side streets, we had no idea where we were.

Fortunately, Isabel hadn't told me the story so I wasn't worried just excited at the speed we were going, but she was.

Hashing in jungle terrain

Hashing through the jungle

5. LIFE AFTER THE ARMY

It was now the end of November 2006 the Chang Mai hash was behind us, we had finished our trip in Thailand. Johnny and I made our way to Australia and family to have a long rest (well as much as is normal for us) until the following March when we returned home. We had been away from home for some time.

A question so many people ask is how did we end up in Dorset.

I had returned to England from Kuwait in 1981 because Pauline our daughter was ready to go to college. We still had our house in the North of England.

Jeremy also asked if he could leave boarding school and attend the excellent local school in Redcar. He never really settled in boarding school, although it did give him a good grounding particularly in all sports, which he became very good at.

Not long after Johnny finished his time with the British Army and got a uniformed contract working in Muscat Oman for the Sultan of Oman's Army, where several of his ex-military comrades were employed.

I spent very happy years in Marske, moving house once again. More on Oman later.

We had always decided we would go back down South when the children's schooling had finished. Johnny suggested Dorset, so I went a couple of times to Bournemouth, and fell in love with the train journey from Bournemouth to Wareham where friends of ours lived. We wanted to be somewhere within the proximity of hills for 'Hashing'. I stayed for a long weekend in Wareham and Wool was suggested, so I drove to Wool and decided to walk the village.

It was a beautiful spring day and I was walking along a residential street and saw a beautiful blue butterfly (I believe native to Dorset) so I followed it not realizing that I was being watched.

The Adonis Blue Butterfly

"What are you doing?"

said Jim Taylor (who I later discovered was his name)

"Chasing butterflies" I said

"No what are you really doing?" he said.

I told him I was looking for a house for sale. We chattered for a bit and he then said he was waiting for his wife and friend to leave his house. They came to the car, I was then asked if I would like to go around the village and he would show me houses for sale, which I did.

After that they said they were going to spend the afternoon at the beach Lulworth Cove and would I like to join them. After a lovely afternoon with my new friends, we went back to their house, where I was invited to afternoon tea. The time was getting on, and they were going to a party in the evening, and asked again would I like to join them, apparently, the party was being given by two brothers who were builders and were both selling their houses. Of course I said 'Yes!'

Later in the evening we were all the best of friends and although I was due to drive back up North the following day for work, I was persuaded to stay an extra day, to view the other brothers' property. I did, and eventually that property was ours!

It took over 6 months for everything to go through, and I was

LIFE AFTER THE ARMY

getting worried because property prices were on the rise again, going up by approximately £1000 per week. But my seller said as I had agreed on a price at the start he would honour it. Johnny at this time had not seen it, but I knew he would be as happy as I.

So, that is how we came to own a large bungalow in Wool.

Two years later Pauline moved from the North to be with us. Jeremy by this time had joined the British Army.

It was now 1987 the time had come to move from Marske-by-sea to Wool in Dorset. We had sold the house. Johnny was on leave so he packed and labelled the boxes as only an Army soldier can. The Removal van arrived and we were ready to go. The only thing was I had to give a month's notice at my place of work, so would have to come back again. The removal men had parked up the night before so when we arrived in Wool they were there waiting for us. We unpacked, stayed the night and then drove back up north.

I was going to stay with my niece Barbara and family in Redcar just two miles away from our previous house until it was time to leave. Our dog Bebe (a King Charles spaniel) was already there waiting for us. Johnny returned to Oman and I settled in. I ended up working and staying another 10 weeks. Johnny had leave every 3 months so this suited us all, and meant it would be close to Christmas time before I left the area.

I decided I would drive the long journey after finishing my last day at the office. The car was packed so it was just a matter of picking up Bebe. I had ahead of me an 8 hour journey but knew the roads would be quieter at this time.

It became a nightmare journey. I was in my estimation about an hour away from Wool in Dorset. It was very late and I was getting tired. Normally when I did this journey, at the Ferndown area (near Bournemouth) I would take the Bournemouth route. But this time a new road and roundabout had been built going towards Dorchester and for some reason I went that way. A big mistake! I didn't know where I was going. Eventually I saw a sign which said Wareham, so I turned left onto the narrow country road. In front of me was a pub (closed of course) called 'Worlds End'. It felt like it! If I had only gone on a few more miles I would have seen the Bere Regis sign a familiar area, but at that time I did not know). So I followed the road to the end. By this time Bebe was whining in the back, thick fog was swirling, and I thought I was lost. The road to my relief came out at a crossing I knew, so I was on the right track and knew it would only be about 20 minutes to reach my destination. Eventually we arrived, by this time it was after 3am. Exhausted I went straight to bed.

Pauline and Jeremy joined me a few days later as did Johnny, we were all to spend Christmas together. It was wonderful all of us discovering the area together. Very shortly after Christmas it was time for Jeremy to return to his Army unit and Pauline back to work at Grinkle Park Hotel and estate near Saltburn in North Yorkshire.

I was then to join Johnny in Oman for 3 months. Our neighbours (Ken and Margaret) kindly said they would come into our house to check it out each day. This was to be one of the worst winters Dorset had experienced for a very long time. We left Heathrow airport just after New Year's Day 1988 in thick snow. Our aircraft was one of the last to be able to take off that day due to the bad weather conditions.

We had only been gone just over a week when we received a phone call from Ken saying we had a water leak, but not to worry the plumber had been called and the water had been switched off, so no need to return just enjoy the holiday – which I did.

In early April when it was close to the time for me to return to UK, Ken turned the water and heating on for me. Disaster! The following morning he went back into the house to find it flooded. Apparently all the pipes had previously unknown to them frozen. I received a frantic phone call asking me to return immediately. It took me a few days to organise a flight back. When I arrived home I could not believe my eyes. Water was still pouring through the kitchen, utility rooms and the living room. Fortunately, because the house was being looked after the insurance covered the considerable damage which was in the thousands. The kitchen was a complete right off, not just the units but all the tiles had come off the walls and there were huge gouges in the plaster.

It took months to be put right, but the Loss Adjuster had been very good. What I didn't know at the time was I could have moved out at the insurance companies expense, but I didn't and lived for 3 months with builders in the house. At the end of it we did get a beautiful kitchen (although nothing had been wrong with the previous one when we moved in). Completely new flooring, curtains carpet were replaced. I would not want to go through that experience again. And as for our new neighbours, it was a terrible trauma for them also. How lucky we were to have them, and we will be forever in their debt.

Work in Dorset

I was very lucky to get an amazing job with The Royal Signals Motorcycle Display Team, The White Helmets, based in Blandford as their Events Co-ordinator and Secretary.

The lapel badge from my time with The White Helmets

Not only was it a wonderful experience, but because of the travelling and long hours, unusual for the Ministry of Defence, Civil Service (who I was working for), they allowed me to take my leave for however long and when convenient for The White Helmets (which was in the winter period when they weren't performing), so that I could join Johnny in Oman.

I stayed with The White Helmets until my retirement in late 2003. To work with 30+ plus young adventurous soldiers and be treated as part of them was certainly a highlight of my life. It would take too long to go into aspects of it, just to say it was often very exciting and never a dull moment.

At that time, we did a lot of TV shows as well as other numerous prestigious events. I have recently been told this 2017 is to be their final year, they are being disbanded. I along with many others think this is a very sad decision. I have been invited to their final reunion party but unfortunately will be unable to attend as I will be in Spain and can't change the dates.

Team photograph from my time with The White Helmets.

LIFE AFTER THE ARMY

Life in the New Millennium

We moved to Weymouth in early 2001 Johnny had finished in Oman and was working in Blandford Camp, as a civilian in the Ministry of Defence for The Royal Signals. He enjoyed the work as it was still related to his military career and he was working with the Military.

Pauline had married Richard some time previously and moved to Croydon in Surrey. Jeremy had left his Army career behind realizing it wasn't really what he wanted, although he had completed 6 years. He then went onto University for 3 years, then worked in London for a while. He brought an apartment in Twickenham, London and then in 2000 moved to Australia where he had an excellent job in Sydney, met and married a beautiful Australian girl Belinda. We now have one teenage granddaughter Jessica in Surrey and three grandsons in Australia.

Now to speak more about Oman. I was so lucky to spend time in Oman such an amazing country and people, only because Johnny had finished his British Military service in 1983. He got a contract with The Sultan of Oman's Army in Muscat. As I said previously, this is where we first discovered Hashing, which although a strenuous way to keep fit, and socialize, it was also one of the best ways to discover places where other people weren't always permitted to go.

Of course, there were sometimes mountains/large hills to be climbed, but that was always a challenge accepted. Many a time I used to moan that the large hills were so difficult, but Johnny always said, everyone found them difficult, but we could all manage them.

Pauline, Richard and Jeremy spent a holiday in Oman with Johnny. They did a lot of travelling whilst there and loved the Country.

We once camped overnight on the beach in a place called Ras Al Hadd with friends. We watched an amazing sight of turtles burying their eggs in the sand, each laying approximately one hundred eggs. The turtles then went back to the sea and wouldn't return again except to lay more eggs another year. We had to be silent with no lights (although the moon was very bright), or the turtles would not appear. We also saw the baby turtles being hatched and making a dash for the sea. They instinctively moved so fast, hundreds of them, they didn't all make it, as predators like foxes or birds were waiting for them.

We had to travel by 4 x 4's vehicles as the road was just a track and quite steep in places. I don't believe a normal car could make it. We went back 10 years later and the site had then become protected and taken over by The Oman Tourist Board, so we couldn't do what we had done in previous years because camping was now highly organised by the Board, and I believe it is now quite expensive to do this. But certainly worth while.

Johnny did a second tour of duty in Oman but this time in Southern Oman a place called Thumrait. When I used to visit, which was very often, I flew into Muscat and stayed overnight in a Company complex and the following day flew in a very small plane to Salalah in the Dhofar province, then one hours journey up the mountain to Thumrait which was an Omani Airbase. Johnny worked very closely with Americans on this base we discovered how different their culture is to ours, but we still have friends to this day.

A typical roadside fruit seller

Me with a banana tree.

In Salalah we picked bananas from the plantations edging on the main roads.

We camped overnight weekends with friends in deserted beaches with turquoise waters (this was the Indian Ocean). We needed 4x4 trucks to access these places because again they were little more than tracks and very steep hills to get there, but it was so worth it.

I once met an Omani lady picking Frankincense which comes from a bush and is a resin – she showed me how she did it and gave me a handful, which had hardened by then. This would then be burnt in an Incense Burner to give off its unique smell.

We did a road trip from Thumrait to Muscat which was about 700 kms, and took about 10 hours. We stayed at a hotel just outside Nizwa.

We spent some time in Nizwa which is a very old walled city, and you feel as though you are going back in time. Before arriving at the hotel, we stopped on the road and discovered an abandoned village, and decided to wander around it.

We were met with a teenage boy about 17 years old I would imagine, and he offered to show us around, he spoke very good English, he told us, when the village became old (the houses were mainly made of mud), the whole village moved to another site within walking distance.

He took us to his house on this site, and invited us to tea, of fruit, and dates, and coffee, which his mother prepared and then left us, we sat on a carpet to eat. These people had so little but their hospitality was considerable.

When we first went to Oman, pavements still hadn't been built, in the villages it was mainly bazaars for shopping. Now the Country has become a highly praised holiday area, and much more built up with several prestigious hotels. We were very lucky to have got it all for free.

We were on our way to Australia in 2010 to spend Christmas with the family and later go onto New Zealand with Belinda (our daughter-in-law's) Mum and Dad who were very good friends of ours. We stopped off in Dubai to stay with Nicki and Noel who had been our friends for many years. They had a house built in Australia and intended to retire there in a few years.

They were going to Townsville where their house was in late January 2011 the following year and asked us if we would visit them there. When we were talking to Jeremy after arriving in Australia he asked if we knew how far it was from Sydney, we didn't and he said it was about four hours by plane.

Anyway, we did go, and were going to spend just a few days before our planned holiday to New Zealand. What we didn't know was a cyclone called Yasi was due to hit Queensland, and mainly the area of Townsville in Queensland. Jeremy said he heard it on the news after he had dropped us off at the airport.

LIFE AFTER THE ARMY

We didn't know about this until the following day, we had gone to a local beauty spot called Alligator Creek, with our friends and some young men were swimming, they came over and asked if we were getting out.

We didn't know what they were talking about, because we had no radio or television in our friend's house, and so the boys told us what to expect. We started to get panic phone calls from the family including Jeremy telling us to immediately get a flight back to Sydney.

We also tried the train station but were unsuccessful all flights and other transport had been cancelled. Our flight back to Sydney had also been cancelled. Nicky and Noel suggested we may not be able to get back to the airport from their house (in case the road was blocked or was flooded), so we would go and stay with Noel's brother in the town.

We went to the supermarkets to get essential food, but they were empty – stripped bare. The shop windows were taped over. It looked like something from the London blitz, that when we realized how serious it was.

We went to Noel's brother's house, where there was another family staying the same as we were. The Cyclone was a Category 5 and hit us on 1st February. We were watching on the TV and the newscasters were telling us to get out, then all of a sudden they said,

"Do not move it's too late, the Cyclone is approaching very quickly and it would be too dangerous to move".

They said:

"We will be with you all the way but have not seen anything as severe as this so don't know what to expect".

At 9 pm that evening we lost all outside contact.

Very scary!

Our hosts had filled the bath with water for emergencies, opened the attic window slightly so the wind would flow through, something to do with pressure I expect. They told us as a last resort we would go into their garage and their car.

The garage was solid and we would be safe there if the roof of the house came off.

LIFE AFTER THE ARMY

Then said we had better all go to bed as we didn't know what we would find in the morning! We then went into a bedroom with sleeping bags on the floor. By this time the wind was howling very loudly.

Later Johnny did manage to sleep, but I couldn't, the only thing I could relate the noise to, as if maybe three planes were flying overhead the whole time on top of each other. It was so loud. The house shook it was horrendous.

Then all of a sudden about 3 am it was silent. This was the 'eye of the storm', turning around – then it all started again.

We went into the kitchen very early in the morning the wind had died down by this time, much to our relief and it was raining. We had been warned not to go out of the house, but late afternoon we were restless and needed some air, so Johnny and I went for a short walk.

Although very serious, we had been so lucky sometime through the night the storm had veered in another direction and although not missed us entirely, the damage wasn't too extensive, and I believe there had only been one casualty.

Even so we didn't stay out long, there were trampolines smashed along the road and other large debris. It was very warm, but the rain was like needles stabbing us and the wind was still very strong.

The following day we were going to try to get a plane back to Sydney, the Airport was now open, it was imperative we left then because only a couple of days later we were due to fly to New Zealand. Part of the road wad flooded but our host knew an alternative route.

What he did say, was he wasn't too worried about the floods, but if there was anything in the road, it may not be a rock so we were not to get out of the car because it could be a crocodile!

Very reassuring!

We did manage to get a priority flight, but we thought when we got to the airport we could have a hot drink, as all power had gone in the house. This wasn't to be as there was no power there either. What a relief to see Jeremy in Sydney to meet us.

Two days later we left for New Zealand, with Faye and Col Belinda's Mum and Dad we arrived at Christchurch and stayed in

LIFE AFTER THE ARMY

the centre of the city, where we were met by our tour operator, for a 2 week coach tour of the Island. We saw the aftermath of the Earthquake from the previous year in Christchurch.

We had a wonderful holiday which included a train journey across the Alpine Pass.

Another highlight was going to an ancient village called Arrowtown where gold was mined. The town was established in 1862 during the height of the gold rush. Cottages were hurriedly constructed with hotels and churches. The village is now a museum, and shows how harsh the life of the early pioneers was. I was allowed to hold a very large nugget of gold.

We returned to Christchurch for our final night before catching our flight back to Sydney. The following morning 22nd February 2011, I received a phone call from our travelling companions asking if we had heard the news, and to turn the television on.

We did so to find there had been another severe earthquake in Christchurch, the hotel that we had stayed in along with others in the same road was severely damaged so much else in the city was also flattened. What a tragedy and how lucky we were to have left the day previous. There had been an earthquake there the previous September, barely time to recover. We were watching it live on TV, the TV station was also a building that we watched go down.

Horrendous!

Some of our friends said to tell them when we are going away and they would know not to book a similar time or trip, as disaster seemed to follow us. Remembering there was the Iranian Revolution, and the Iran/Iraq war, to name just a few.

Since living in Dorset I have made so many great friends, but one particular friend who I can't finish this book without mentioning is Carol, we have been friends for over 30 years and spent so much time together and done so much, laughed and cried, and I know if ever I needed her she would be there for me, as I would her. We both have a mutual interest in the late 1950s and 1960s bands, and go to many music shows together.

Johnny calls us 'Groupies', any opportunity we had to dance/jive even in the streets we did, and still do. There was one instance when some years ago whilst Johnny was still in Oman, 'Status Quo' were doing a show in Bournemouth just before Christmas.

LIFE AFTER THE ARMY

My air tickets had been booked by Johnny's Company to travel to Oman before this particular show was due – well I couldn't miss the 'Quo', so I changed the date of them. The show was fantastic and well worth the hassle I was going to receive. Unfortunately, when I did arrive in Oman – I was not popular, the Company (and it goes without saying nor was Johnny...) were none too pleased when I arrived because I had changed the flight dates, and somebody would have been at the Airport in Muscat to greet me, and escort me to my accommodation before I was to catch another flight to Salalah the following day.

I arrived on Christmas Eve just in time for the annual Christmas Dinner, and to cap it all I gave everybody a very bad cold or flu.

Johnny and I are now in our seventies and have been married over fifty very happy years. We had a huge party on that Anniversary with 100 friends and family.

Our Fiftieth Wedding Party

I wanted to wear a dress from the 1960s, so managed to buy one. But when I told my daughter she said I needed to wear something more elegant.

LIFE AFTER THE ARMY

So, I brought another dress to suit the occasion, but what I didn't tell her was I would change after all the speeches were over and it was time for the dancing. So, I changed and my 1960s dress was a huge success, and I was able to dance better in it.

Me dancing at our Fiftieth Anniversary – Johnny in the background

We do now spend some time in Australia with our family, but still keep up with all our friends in UK and all over the world. And of course, 'Hashing' is still a large part of our life with Hardy's Hash in Weymouth.

This is just a sample of some of the things we have done and are still doing with our life. Yes, I do have a life outside Hashing. Weymouth is the longest we have lived anywhere, and we love it and have no intention of moving on!

Printed in Great Britain
by Amazon